Spelling and Writing

Table of Contents

Glossary	2
Spelling: Long i and long a	3
Writing: Finding out about pronouns	4
Spelling: Changing vowels with a final e	5
Writing: Using pronouns correctly	6
Spelling: Rhyming and defining words	7
Writing: Writing poetry	8
Spelling: Spelling possessive pronouns	9
Review	10
Spelling: Spelling long o and long e	11
Spelling: Sorting out homophones	12
Spelling: Making new words	13
Spelling: Using different forms of verbs	14
Writing: Being specific	15
Spelling: Finishing a crossword puzzle	16
Review	17
Spelling: Spelling words with diagraphs	18
Writing: Choosing "joining words"	19
Spelling: Cracking the code	20
Writing: Combining ideas	21
Spelling: Searching for synonyms	22
Writing: Knowing when to stop	23
Spelling: Practicing proofreading	24
Review	25
Writing: Writing support sentences	26
Spelling: Sounding out syllables	27
Writing: Putting ideas in order	28
Spelling: Meeting word families	29
Writing: Building paragraphs	30
Spelling: Using plurals in math	31
Review	32

Copyright © 1994 American Education Publishing Co.

Glossary

Adjectives. Words that describe nouns and pronouns.
Adverb. Words that tell something about a verb.
Apostrophe. A punctuation mark that shows possession (Kim's hat) or takes the place of missing letters in a word (isn't).
Digraph. Two consonant letters pronounced as one consonant sound.
Fact. A true statement. Something that can be proved.
Homophones. Words that sound alike but have different spellings and meanings.
Joining Words (Conjunctions). Words that join sentences or combine ideas.
Metaphor. A comparison without the words **like** or **as**.
Noun. A word that names a person, place, or thing.
Opinion. What someone thinks or believes.
Paragraph. A group of sentences that tells about one main idea.
Plural. A word that refers to more than one thing.
Prefix. One or two syllables added to the beginning of a word to change its meaning.
Pronoun. A word that can be used in place of a noun.
Question. A sentence that ask something.
Simile. A comparison using the words **like** or **as**.
Singular. A words that refers to only one thing.
Subject. A word or several words that tell whom or what a sentence is about.
Suffix. One or two syllables added to the end of a word.
Synonym. A word that means the same thing as another word.
Verb. The action word in a sentence; the word that tells what something does or that something exists.

Spelling and Writing

Name: _____

Spelling Words With Long i And Long a

Long **i** is written /ī/. The words in this lesson spell /ī/ two ways: **i**-consonant-**e** as in h**i**d**e** and **y** as in m**y**. The vowel /ī/ can also be spelled **i** as in k**i**nd and **igh** as in fl**igh**t.

Long **a** is written /ā/. The words in this lesson spell /ā/ **a**-consonant-**e** as in pl**a**t**e** and **ai** as in p**ai**n. The vowel /ā/ can also be spelled **a** as in **a**ble and **ay** as in d**ay**.

Directions: Use words from the word box in these exercises.

| style | bathe | faith | title | dye | pride | daily | praise | spite | scrape |

1. Write each word in the row that has its vowel sound.

/ī/ _____ _____ _____ _____ _____

/ā/ _____ _____ _____ _____ _____

2. Say the word on the left. Then circle the two other words in that row that have the same vowel sound.

faith	date	crack	play	jam
spite	high	drill	quilt	sly
bathe	bath	social	raid	ape
style	clay	twice	while	still

3. Finish these sentences, using a word with the vowel sound given. Use each word from the word box only once.

The /ī/ _____ of clothes changes every year.

To stay clean, we all need to /ā/ _____ /ā/ _____ .

I liked the book in /ī/ _____ of its /ī/ _____ .

However, the newspaper review did not /ā/ _____ the book.

Why did she /ī/ _____ her hair that color?

Even though we were having problems finishing our project, our teacher said she had /ā/ _____ that we could do it.

Copyright © 1994 American Education Publishing Co.

Spelling and Writing

Name: _____

Finding Out About Pronouns

A pronoun is a word that is used in place of a noun. Instead of repeating a noun again and again, we can use a pronoun. Here are some common pronouns:

I	we	you	he	she	they	it
me	us	your	him	her	them	its
my	our		his		their	

Each pronoun takes the place of a certain noun. If the noun is singular, the pronoun needs to be singular. If the noun is plural, the pronoun should be plural.

Like this: John told **his** parents **he** would be late. The girls said **they** would ride **their** bikes.

Directions: In the sentences below draw a line from the noun to the pronoun that takes its place.

Like this: Gail needs the salt. Please pass it to her.

1. The workers had faith they would finish the house in time.

2. Kathy fell and scraped her knees. She put bandages on them.

3. The teacher told the students he wanted to see their papers.

Directions: Cross out some nouns and write the pronoun that could be used.

Like this: Dan needed a book for ~~Dan's~~ his book report.

1. Brian doesn't care about the style of Brian's clothes.

2. Joy dyed Joy's jeans to make the jeans dark blue.

3. Faith said Faith was tired of sharing a bedroom with Faith's two sisters. Faith wanted a room of Faith's own.

4. Bathe babies carefully so the soap doesn't get in the babies' eyes and make the babies cry.

5. When the children held up the children's pictures, we could see the pride in the children's eyes.

Copyright © 1994 American Education Publishing Co.

4

Spelling and Writing

Name: _____

Changing Vowels With A Final e

Adding **e** to the end of some words changes a short vowel to a long vowel.

Like this: mat - mat**e**   sit - sit**e**

Directions: Add **e** to the end of these words to make new words. Then write /ī/ or /ā/ to show the long vowel in the new word. The first one is done for you.

mad	made ā	bit	_____
dim	_____	tap	_____
hid	_____	pin	_____
fat	_____	past	_____
fin	_____	spit	_____
kit	_____	bath	_____
win	_____	rip	_____
hat	_____	scrap	_____
rid	_____	twin	_____

Directions: Answer these questions with words from the word box.

| style | bathe | faith | title | dye | pride | daily | praise | spite | scrape |

1. Which words are pronounced this way?

/stīl/ _____   /prās/ _____

/skrāp/ _____   /dī/ _____

/prīd/ _____   /spīt/ _____

2. Which word has a **y** that is not pronounced /ī/? _____

5

Copyright © 1994 American Education Publishing Co.

Spelling and Writing

Name: _____

Using Pronouns Correctly

Sometimes people have trouble matching nouns and pronouns. Here is an example: A teacher should always be fair to their students.

Teacher is **singular**, but **their** is **plural**, so they don't match. Still we can't say "A teacher should always be fair to his students" because teachers are both men and women. "His or her students" sounds awkward.

One easy way to handle this problem is to make teacher plural so it will match their: Teachers should always be fair to their students.

Directions: Correct the pronoun problems in these sentences by writing in a different pronoun or by making the noun plural. (If you make the noun plural, make the verb plural, too.) Then draw a line from the noun to its correct pronoun.

Like this: Ron's school won ~~their~~ *its* basketball game.

You can tell if ~~a cat is~~ *cats are* angry by watching their tails.

1. A student should try to praise their friends' strong points.

2. The group finished their work on time in spite of the deadline.

3. A parent usually has a lot of faith in their children.

4. The company paid their workers once a week.

5. The train made their daily run from Chicago to Detroit.

6. Each student should have a title on their papers.

Directions: Finish these sentences by writing in the correct pronouns.

1. Simon fell out of the tree and scraped _____ arm.

2. The citizens felt a deep pride in _____ community.

3. Harry and Sheila wear _____ hair in the same style.

4. I dyed some shirts, but _____ didn't turn out right.

5. The nurse showed the mother how to bathe _____ baby.

6. Our school made $75 from _____ carnival.

Copyright © 1994 American Education Publishing Co.

Spelling and Writing

Name: _____

Rhyming And Defining Words

Directions: Write the word from the word box that rhymes with each of these. (Some words are not used, and some are used more than once.)

| style | bathe | faith | title | dye | pride | daily | praise | spite | scrape |

cape _____   right _____

pile _____   tried _____

gaily _____   pie _____

days _____   dyed _____

dial _____   graze _____

cry _____   write _____

grape _____   fly _____

bite _____   tape _____

tied _____   trays _____

Directions: Write the word from the word box that matches each definition.

1. A strong belief: _____

2. A certain way of doing something: _____

3. The name of a book: _____

4. Every day: _____

5. One way to get clean: _____

6. To say what you like about something: _____

7. A feeling of success: _____

8. To change the color: _____

Writing Poetry

Directions: For the first group of poems below, both lines rhyme. Finish each poem, using one of the rhyming words given, another one from page 7, or one you think of yourself.

Like this:

mile	Kevin James has a certain style.
pile	
dial	To get his way, he'd walk a mile.

ape	Mindy Lou got a very bad scrape!
grape	
cape	_____

hide	Sometimes you have to swallow your pride
fried	
cried	_____

lays	One dark day I needed some praise
plays	
graze	_____

Directions: Each poem in this second group has four lines. The second and fourth lines rhyme. Finish these poems with the words given or others.

Like this:

cape	Kenny skidded on his bike
tape	And got himself all **scraped**.
grape	Now his bike has a flat tire,
	And his whole leg is **taped**.

I	I put some water in a bucket
cry	And then threw in some **dye**.
my	
	_____

file	Kelly got her hair cut,
dial	But I don't like the **style**.
Nile	
	_____

ride	When Billy didn't win the race,
hide	It really hurt his **pride**.
cried	
	_____

Spelling and Writing

Name: _____

Spelling Possessive Pronouns

A possessive pronoun shows ownership. Pronouns can be possessive, just like nouns. Instead of writing "That is Jill's book," we can write "That is her book" or "That is hers." Instead of "I lost my pencil," we can write "I lost mine." Use these possessive pronouns when you name what is possessed.

    my (book)   our (car)   your (hat)   his (leg)   her (hair)   their (group)   its (team)

Use these possessive pronouns when you don't name what is possessed:
    mine   ours   yours   his   hers   theirs

Did you notice that possessive pronouns don't use apostrophes?

Directions: Finish these sentences by writing in the possesssive pronouns. Make sure you don't use apostrophes.

Like this: This book belongs to Jon. It is ____his____ .

1. I brought my lunch. Did you bring _____ ?

2. I can't do my homework. I wonder if Nancy figured out _____ .

3. Jason saved his candy bar, but I ate _____ .

4. Our team finished our project, but they didn't finish _____ .

5. They already have their assignment. When will we get _____ ?

Some people confuse the possessive pronoun **its** with the contraction for **it is**, which is spelled **it's**. The apostrophe in **it's** shows that the **i** in **is** has been left out.

Directions: Write **its** or **it's** in each sentence below.

Like this: The book has lost ____its____ cover.   ____It's____ going to rain soon.

1. _____ nearly time to go.

2. The horse has hurt _____ leg.

3. Every nation has _____ share of problems.

4. What is _____ name?

5. I think _____ too warm to snow.

6. The teacher said _____ up to us.

Spelling and Writing

Name: _____

Review

Directions: Finish the poems below. Rhyme the first line with the third line and the second line with the fourth line.

Like this: I know a title for a **book**.
I've known of it for **ages**.
The part that really has me **shook**
Is how to fill the **pages**.

I have a dog I love to **praise**.
His tricks will just amaze **you**.

_____

_____

My favorite jeans were getting **old**
And so I bought some **dye**.

_____

_____

Directions: Write sentences for five of the words in the word box. Include at least one pronoun in each sentence. Draw a line from each pronoun to its noun. (Make sure the pronoun is plural if the noun is plural and remember not to use apostrophes in possessive pronouns.)

| style | bathe | faith | title | dye | pride | daily | praise | spite | scrape |

Like this: Pam has faith in her project in spite of its problems.

1. _____
2. _____
3. _____
4. _____
5. _____

Spelling and Writing

Name: _____

Spelling Words With Long o And Long e

Long **o** is written /ō/. The words in this lesson spell /ō/ two ways: **oa** as in b**oa**t and **o**-consonant-**e** as in h**ope**. This vowel can also be spelled **o** as in **o**pen, **ow** as in gl**ow**, and **ew** as in s**ew**.

Long **e** is written /ē/. The words in this lesson spell /ē/ with **e** as in m**e**, **ee** as in s**ee**n, and **ea** as in pl**ea**se. This vowel can also be spelled **ie** as in bel**ie**ve.

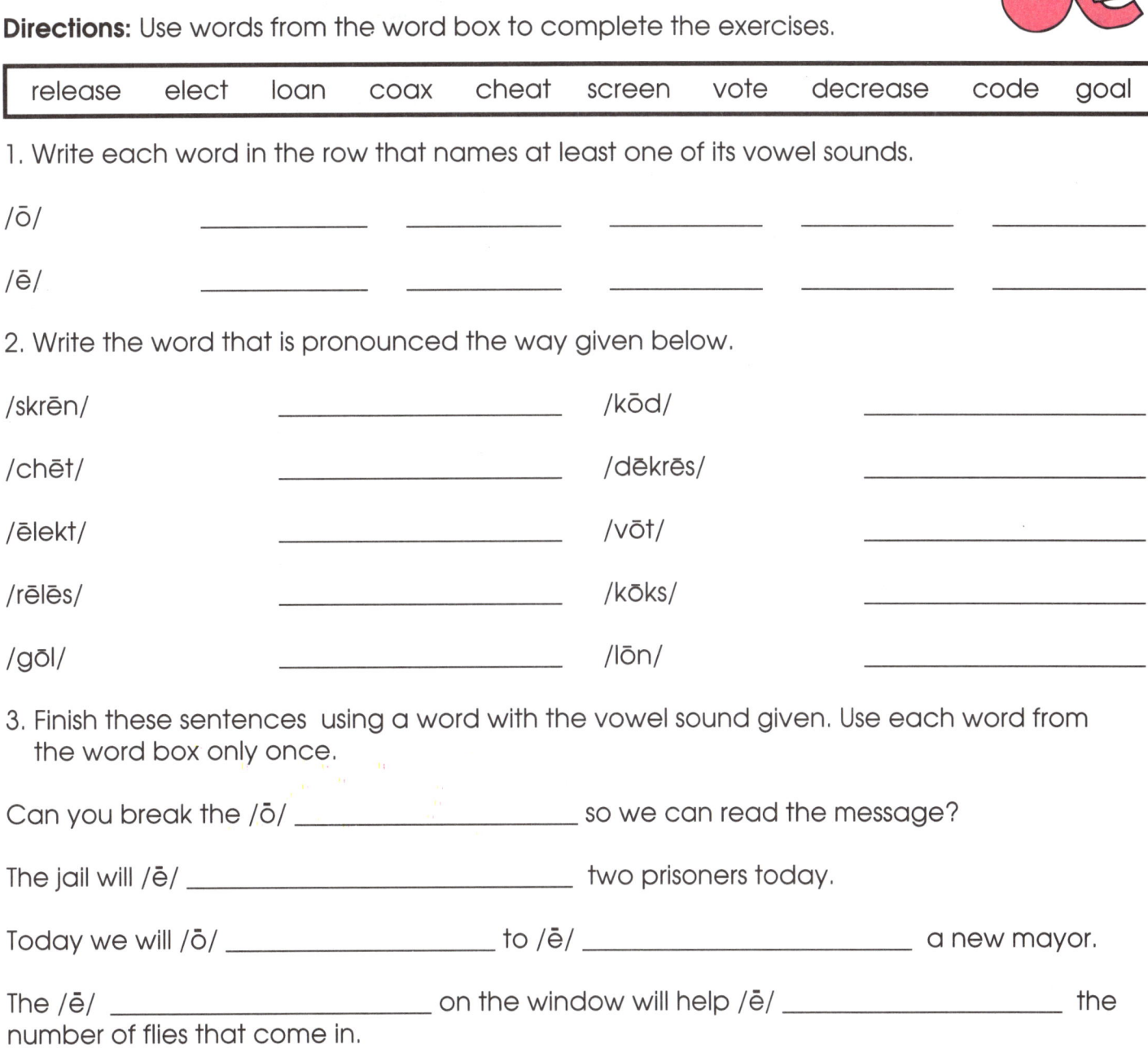

Directions: Use words from the word box to complete the exercises.

| release | elect | loan | coax | cheat | screen | vote | decrease | code | goal |

1. Write each word in the row that names at least one of its vowel sounds.

/ō/ _____ _____ _____ _____ _____

/ē/ _____ _____ _____ _____ _____

2. Write the word that is pronounced the way given below.

/skrēn/ _____   /kōd/ _____

/chēt/ _____   /dēkrēs/ _____

/ēlekt/ _____   /vōt/ _____

/rēlēs/ _____   /kōks/ _____

/gōl/ _____   /lōn/ _____

3. Finish these sentences using a word with the vowel sound given. Use each word from the word box only once.

Can you break the /ō/ _____ so we can read the message?

The jail will /ē/ _____ two prisoners today.

Today we will /ō/ _____ to /ē/ _____ a new mayor.

The /ē/ _____ on the window will help /ē/ _____ the number of flies that come in.

You won't reach your /ō/ _____ if you /ē/ _____ .

11

Copyright © 1994 American Education Publishing Co.

SPELLING AND WRITING

Name: _____

Sorting Out Homophones

Homophones are words that sound alike but have different spellings and different meanings. The words no and know are homophones. They sound alike, but their spellings and meanings are very different.

Directions: Use the words in the word box for these exercises.

hour	wring	knot	whole	knew
wrap	knight	piece	write	

1. Write each word from the word box beside its homophone.

peace _____   new _____   ring _____

hole _____   rap _____   night _____

not _____   right _____   our _____

2. Write the three words above that have a silent k. _____ _____ _____

3. Write the one word with a silent h. _____ _____ _____

4. Which four words have a silent w? _____ _____ _____ _____

5. Rewrite each sentence, using the correct homophones.

By the time knight fell, I new she was knot coming.

_____

I would never have any piece until I new the hole story.

_____

He spent an our righting down what had happened.

_____

I could see write through the whole in the night's armor.

_____

Spelling and Writing   12

Copyright © 1994 American Education Publishing Co.

Spelling and Writing

Name: _____

Making New Words

Directions: Make new words from old ones by adding and subtracting short vowels (/a/, /e/, /i/, /o/, and /u/), long vowels (/ī/, /ā/, /ō/, and /ē/), and consonants. The spelling of some words will change quite a bit with the new vowel. (Some of the answers are on pages 3 or 11.)

Like this:

    Pete   -   /ē/ + /e/ =   _pet_____

1. boat   -   /b/ + /v/ = _____
2. kid   -   /i/ + /ō/ = _____
3. lean   -   /ē/ + /ō/ = _____
4. kicks   -   /i/ + /ō/ = _____
5. gull   -   /u/ + /ō/ = _____
6. steak   -   /ā/ + /o/ = _____
7. line   -   /ī/ + /ō/ = _____
8. don't   -   /ō/ + /e/ = _____
9. dolly   -   /o/ + /ā/ = _____
10. prayed   -   /ā/ + /ī/ = _____
11. still   -   /i/ + /ī/ = _____
12. lake   -   /ā/ + /a/ = _____
13. rents   -   /e/ + /i/ = _____
14. rob   -   /o/ + /ō/ = _____
15. like   -   /ī/ + /ā/ = _____
16. gill   -   /i/ + /ō/ = _____
17. lane   -   /ā/ + /ō/ = _____

Spelling and Writing

Name: _____

Using Different Forms Of Verbs

To explain what is happening right now, we can use a "plain" verb or we can use **is** or **are** and add **-ing** to the verb.

Like this: We eat. We **are** eat**ing**.

Remember that when a verb already ends with **e**, drop the **e** before adding another ending.

Like this: He serves. He **is** serv**ing**.

Directions: Finish each sentence with the correct form of the verb, telling what is happening right now. Read carefully, as some sentences already have **is** or **are**.

Like this: Scott is (loan) ____loaning____ Jenny his math book.

Jenny (like) ____likes____ reading better than math.

1. The court is (release) _____ the prisoner early.

2. Jack and Jill (write) _____ their notes in code.

3. Are you (vote) _____ for Henry?

4. The girls are (coax) _____ the dog into the bathtub.

5. This nation (elect) _____ a president every four years.

6. My little brother (cheat) _____ when we play Monopoly.

7. Is she (hide) _____ behind the screen?

To explain what already happened, we can add **-ed** to many verbs or we can use **was** or **were** and add **-ing** to the verb.

Like this: I watch**ed**. I **was** watch**ing**.

Directions: As you did above, write in the correct forms of the verbs. This time, tell what already happened.

Like this: We (walk) ____walked____ there yesterday. They were (talk) ____talking____.

8. The government was (decrease) _____ our taxes.

9. Was anyone (cheat) _____ in this game?

10. We were (try) _____ to set goals for the project.

Spelling and Writing

Name: _____

Being Specific

Our writing is clearer and more interesting when we use "German shepherd" instead of "dog" and when we write "lemon pie" instead of "dessert." Specific words tell readers what we really mean.

Directions: Write a more specific word or words for each general one. The first one is done for you.

store   _K-Mart_   building   _____

game   _____   TV show   _____

pet   _____   worker   _____

car   _____   dessert   _____

bird   _____   clothing   _____

Directions: Rewrite these sentences using more specific words, and add adjectives and adverbs so the reader knows exactly what you mean. Mark at least one adjective (ADJ) and one adverb (ADV) in each of your sentences.

                         ADJ   ADJ   ADV

Like this: The tree fell down. The ancient oak in our front yard was knocked down by high winds.

1. The road led to a town.
_____

2. The girl heard a sound.
_____

3. The boy finished his project.
_____

4. The flower was pretty.
_____

5. The baby made a mess.
_____

6. Pat rode her new bike.
_____

Copyright © 1994 American Education Publishing Co.

Spelling and Writing

Name: _____

Finishing A Crossword Puzzle

Directions: Write the word to match each definition in the spaces that start with the same number. (If you are having trouble spelling the words, they are in the word box on page 11.)

Across
2. Not to follow the rules
4. To let something go
6. The front of a television
8. To take part in an election
9. To lend someone something
10. To beg

Down
1. To make something smaller
3. Symbols
5. Something you want to reach
7. To select someone for a certain position

Copyright © 1994 American Education Publishing Co.

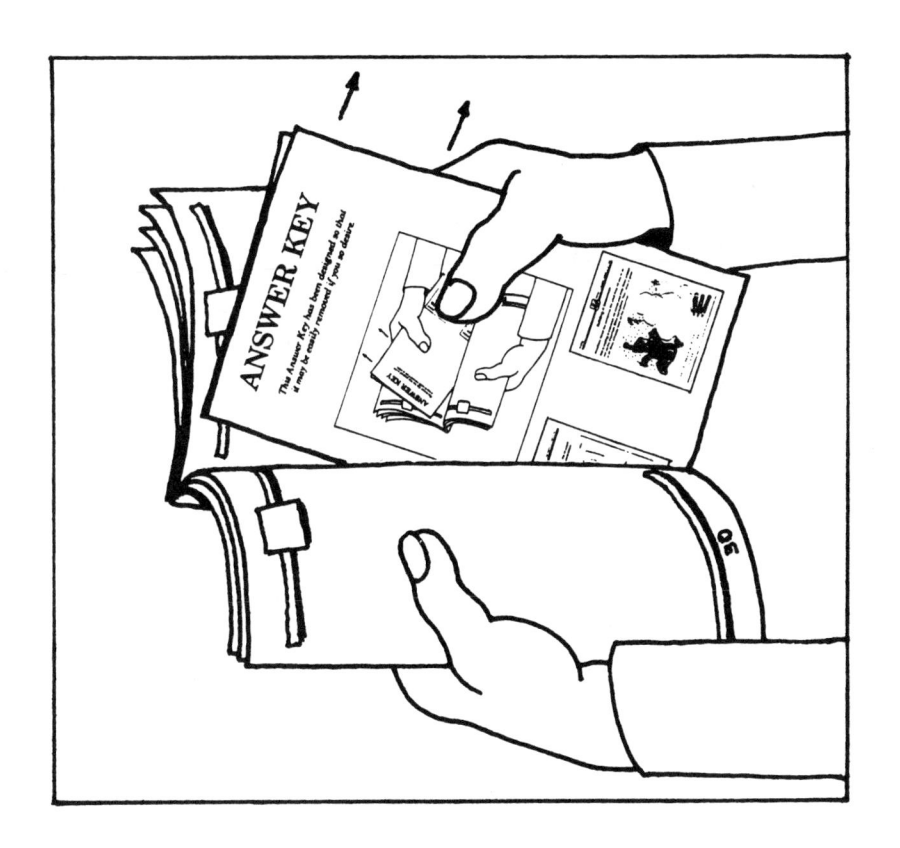

ANSWER KEY

This Answer Key has been designed so that it may be easily removed if you so desire.

GRADE 5 SPELLING & WRITING

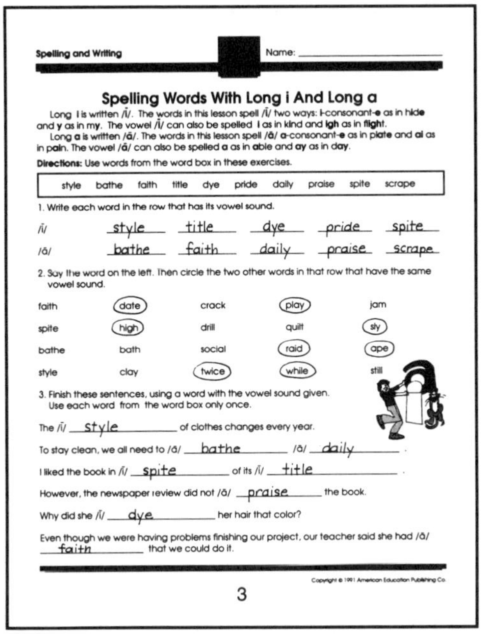

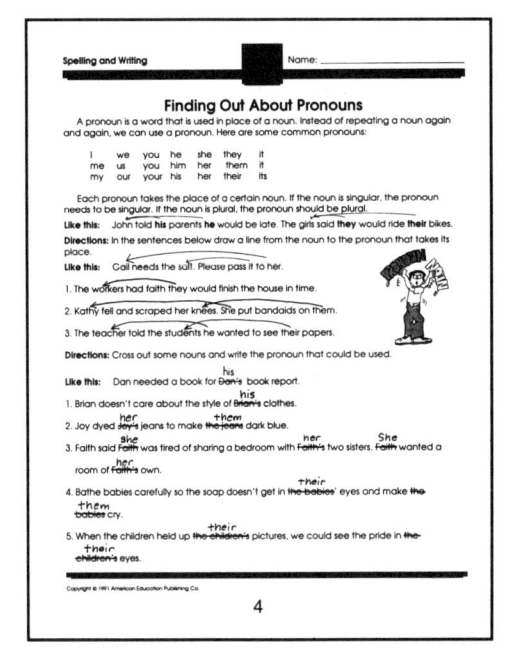

Changing Vowels With A Final e

Adding **e** to the end of some words changes a short vowel to a long vowel.
Like this: mat - mate   sit - site

Directions: Add **e** to the end of these words to make new words. Then write /ī/ or /ā/ to show the long vowel in the new word. The first one is done for you.

mad	made ā	bit	bite ī
dim	dime ī	tap	tape ā
hid	hide ī	pin	pine ī
fat	fate ā	past	paste ā
fin	fine ī	spit	spite ī
kit	kite ī	bath	bathe ā
win	wine ī	rip	ripe ī
hat	hate ā	scrap	scrape ā
rid	ride ī	twin	twine ī

Directions: Answer these questions with words from the word box.

| style | bathe | faith | title | dye | pride | daily | praise | spite | scrape |

1. Which words are pronounced this way?

/stīl/ __style__ /prās/ __praise__
/skrāp/ __scrape__ /dī/ __dye__
/prīd/ __pride__ /spīt/ __spite__

2. Which word has a **y** that is not pronounced /ī/? __daily__

Using Pronouns Correctly

Sometimes people have trouble matching nouns and pronouns. Here is an example:
A teacher should always be fair to their students.

Teacher is singular, but their is plural, so they don't match. Still, we can't say "A teacher should always be fair to his students" because teachers are both men and women. "His or her students" sounds awkward.

One easy way to handle this problem is to make teacher plural so it will match their:
Teachers should always be fair to their students.

Directions: Correct the pronoun problems in these sentences by writing in a different pronoun or by making the noun plural. (If you make the noun plural, make the verb plural, too.) Then draw a line from the noun to its correct pronoun.

Like this:
Ron's school won their basketball game. → its
You can tell if a cat is angry by watching their tails. → cats are
1. A student should try to praise their friends' strong points. → his/her
2. The group finished their work on time in spite of the deadline. → its
3. Parents usually has a lot of faith in their children. → have
4. The company paid their workers once a week. → its
5. The train made their daily run from Chicago to Detroit. → its
6. Each student should have a title on their papers. → his/her

Directions: Finish these sentences by writing in the correct pronouns.

1. Simon fell out of the tree and scraped __his__ arm.
2. The citizens felt a deep pride in __their__ community.
3. Harry and Sheila wear __their__ hair in the same style.
4. I dyed some shirts, but __they__ didn't turn out right.
5. The nurse showed the mother how to bathe __her__ baby.
6. Our school made $75 from __its__ carnival.

Rhyming And Defining Words

Directions: Write the word from the word box that rhymes with each of these. (Some words are not used, and the second are used more than once.)

| style | bathe | faith | title | dye | pride | daily | praise | spite | scrape |

cape	scrape	right	spite
pile	style	tried	pride
gaily	daily	pie	dye
days	praise	dyed	pride
dial	style	graze	praise
cry	dye	write	spite
grape	scrape	fly	dye
bite	spite	tape	scrape
tied	pride	trays	praise

Directions: Write the word from the word box that matches each definition.

1. A strong belief: __faith__
2. A certain way of doing something: __style__
3. The name of a book: __title__
4. Every day: __daily__
5. One way to get clean: __bathe__
6. To say what you like about something: __praise__
7. A feeling of success: __pride__
8. To change the color: __dye__

Writing Poetry

Directions: For the first group of poems below, both lines rhyme. Finish each poem, using one of the rhyming words given, another one from page 13, or one you think of yourself.

Like this:
mile / pile / dial
Kevin James has a certain style.
To get his way, he'd walk a mile.

ape / grape / cape
Mindy Lou got a very bad scrape!
__poem completions will vary__

hide / fried / cried
Som-times you have to swallow your pride
_____

lays / plays / graze
One dark day I needed some praise
_____

Directions: Each poem in this second group has four lines. The second and fourth lines rhyme. Finish these poems with the words given or others.

Like this:
cape / tape / grape
Kenny skidded on his bike
And got himself all **scraped**.
Now his bike has a flat tire,
And his whole leg is **taped**.

I / cry / my
I put some water in a bucket
And then threw in some **dye**.
__poem completions will vary__

file / dial / Nile
Kelly got her hair cut,
But I don't like the **style**.
_____

ride / hide / cried
When Billy didn't win the race,
It really hurt his **pride**.
_____

Spelling Possessive Pronouns

A possessive pronoun shows ownership. Pronouns can be possessive, just like nouns. Instead of writing "That is Jill's book," we can write "That is her book" or "That is hers." Instead of "I lost my pencil," we can write "I lost mine." Use these possessive pronouns when you name what is possessed:
  my (book) our (car) your (hat) his (leg) her (hair) their (group) its (team)

Use these possessive pronouns when you don't name what is possessed:
  mine ours yours his hers theirs

Did you notice that possessive pronouns don't use apostrophes?

Directions: Finish these sentences by writing in the possessive pronouns. Make sure you don't use apostrophes.

Like this: This book belongs to Jon. It is __his__.

1. I brought my lunch. Did you bring __yours__?
2. I can't do my homework. I wonder if Nancy figured out __hers__.
3. Jason saved his candy bar, but I ate __mine__.
4. Our team finished our project, but they didn't finish __theirs__.
5. They already have their assignment. When will we get __ours__?

Some people confuse the possessive pronoun **its** with the contraction for **it is**, which is spelled **it's**. The apostrophe in **it's** shows that the **i** in **is** has been left out.

Directions: Write **its** or **it's** in each sentence below.

Like this: The book has lost __its__ cover. __It's__ going to rain soon.

1. __It's__ nearly time to go.
2. The horse has hurt __its__ leg.
3. Every nation has __its__ share of problems.
4. What is __its__ name?
5. I think __it's__ too warm to snow.
6. The teacher said __it's__ up to us.

Review

Directions: Finish the poems below. Rhyme the first line with the third line and the second line with the fourth line.

Like this:
I know a title for a **book**.
I've known of it for **ages**.
The part that really has me **shook**
Is how to fill the **pages**.

I have a dog I love to **praise**.
His tricks will just amaze **you**.
__poem completions will vary__

My favorite jeans were getting **old**
And so I bought some **dye**.
_____

Directions: Write sentences for eight of the words in the word box. Include at least one pronoun in each sentence. Draw a line from each pronoun to its noun. (Make sure the pronoun is plural if the noun is plural and remember not to use apostrophes in possessive pronouns.)

| style | bathe | faith | title | dye | pride | daily | praise | spite | scrape |

Like this: Pam has faith in her project in spite of its problems.

1. __sentences will vary__
2. _____
3. _____
4. _____
5. _____

Spelling Words With Long o And Long e

Long **o** is written /ō/. The words in this lesson spell /ō/ two ways: **oa** as in **boat** and **o-consonant-e** as in **hope**. This vowel can also be spelled **o** as in **open**, **ow** as in **glow**, and **ew** as in **sew**.
Long **e** is written /ē/. The words in this lesson spell /ē/ with **e** as in **me**, **ee** as in **seen**, and **ea** as in **please**. This vowel can also be spelled **ie** as in **believe**.
Directions: Use words from the word box to complete the exercises.

| release | elect | loan | coax | cheat | screen | vote | decrease | code | goal |

1. Write each word in the row that names at least one of its vowel sounds.

/ō/   loan   coax   vote   code   goal
/ē/   release   elect   screen   decrease   cheat

2. Write the word that is pronounced the way given below.

/skrēn/   screen   /kōd/   code
/chēt/   cheat   /dēkrēs/   decrease
/ēlekt/   elect   /vōt/   vote
/rēlēs/   release   /kōks/   coax
/gōl/   goal   /lōn/   loan

3. Finish these sentences, using a word with the vowel sound given. Use each word from the word box only once.

Can you break the /ō/ __code__ so we can read the message?
The jail will /ē/ __release__ two prisoners today.
Today we will /ō/ __vote__ to /ē/ __elect__ a new mayor.
The /ē/ __screen__ on the window will help /ē/ __decrease__ the number of flies that come in.
You won't reach your /ō/ __goal__ if you /ē/ __cheat__.

11

Using Different Forms Of Verbs

To explain what is happening right now, we can use a "plain" verb or we can use **is** or **are** and add **-ing** to the verb.
Like this: We eat. We are eating.
Remember that when a verb already ends with **e**, drop the **e** before adding another ending.
Like this: He serves. He is serving.
Directions: Finish each sentence with the correct form of the verb, telling what is happening right now. Read carefully, as some sentences already have **is** or **are**.
Like this: Scott is (loan) __loaning__ Jenny his math book.
           Jenny (like) __likes__ reading better than math.

1. The court is (release) __releasing__ the prisoner early.
2. Jack and Jill (write) __write / are writing__ their notes in code.
3. Are you (vote) __voting__ for Henry?
4. The girls are (coax) __coaxing__ the dog into the bathtub.
5. This nation (elect) __elects__ a president every four years.
6. My little brother (cheat) __cheats__ when we play Monopoly.
7. Is she (hide) __hiding__ behind the screen?

To explain what already happened, we can add **-ed** to many verbs or we can use **was** or **were** and add **-ing** to the verb.
Like this: I watched. I was watching.
Directions: As you did above, write in the correct forms of the verbs. This time, tell what already happened.
Like this: We (walk) __walked__ there yesterday. They were (talk) __talking__.

8. The government was (decrease) __decreasing__ our taxes.
9. Was anyone (cheat) __cheating__ in this game?
10. We were (try) __trying__ to set goals for the project.

14

Sorting Out Homophones

Homophones are words that sound alike but have different spellings and different meanings. The words **no** and **know** are homophones. They sound alike, but their spellings and meanings are very different.
Directions: Use the words in the word box for these exercises.

| hour | wring | knot | whole | knew |
| wrap | knight | piece | write |

1. Write each word from the word box beside its homophone.

peace   __piece__   new   __knew__   ring   __wring__
hole   __whole__   rap   __wrap__   night   __knight__
not   __knot__   right   __write__   our   __hour__

2. Write the three words above that have a silent k. __knew__ __knight__ __knot__
3. Write the one word with a silent h. __hour__
4. Which four words have a silent w? __whole__ __write__ __wrap__ __wring__
5. Rewrite each sentence, using the correct homophones.

By the time knight fell, I new she was not coming.
__By the time night fell, I knew she was not coming.__

I would never have any piece until I new the hole story.
__I would never have any peace until I knew the whole story.__

He spent an our righting down what had happened.
__He spent an hour writing down what had happened.__

I could see write through the whole in the night's armor.
__I could see right through the hole in the knight's armor.__

12

Being Specific

Our writing is clearer and more interesting when we use "German shepherd" instead of "dog" and when we write "lemon pie" instead of "dessert." Specific words tell readers what we really mean.
Directions: Write a more specific word or words for each general one. The first one is done for you.

store   __K-Mart__   building _____
game   __responses will vary__   TV show _____
pet   _____   worker _____
car   _____   dessert _____
bird   _____   clothing _____

Directions: Rewrite these sentences, using more specific words and adding adjectives and adverbs so the reader knows exactly what you mean.
Mark at least one adjective (ADJ) and one adverb (ADV) in each of your sentences. 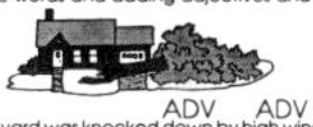
                         ADJ   ADJ   ADV
Like this: The tree fell down. The ancient oak in our front yard was knocked down by high winds.

1. The road led to a town. __Sentences will vary__
2. The girl heard a sound.
3. The boy finished his project.
4. The flower was pretty.
5. The baby made a mess.
6. Pat rode her new bike.

15

Making New Words

Directions: Make new words from old ones by adding and subtracting short vowels (/a/, /e/, /i/, /o/, and /u/), long vowels (/ā/, /ē/, /ī/, /ō/, and /ē/), and consonants. The spelling of some words will change quite a bit with the new vowel. (All of the answers are on page 1, 9, or 17.)

Like this:
Pete   - /ē/ + /e/ =   __pet__
1. boat   - /b/ + /v/ =   __vote__
2. kid   - /i/ + /ō/ =   __code__
3. lean   - /ē/ + /ō/ =   __loan or lone__
4. kicks   - /i/ + /ō/ =   __coax__
5. gull   - /u/ + /ō/ =   __goal__
6. steak   - /ā/ + /o/ =   __stock__
7. line   - /ī/ + /ō/ =   __loan or lone__
8. don't   - /ō/ + /e/ =   __dent__
9. dolly   - /o/ + /ā/ =   __daily__
10. prayed   - /ā/ + /ī/ =   __pride__
11. still   - /i/ + /ī/ =   __style__
12. lake   - /ā/ + /a/ =   __lack__
13. rents   - /e/ + /i/ =   __rinse__
14. rob   - /o/ + /ō/ =   __robe__
15. like   - /ī/ + /ā/ =   __lake__
16. gill   - /i/ + /ō/ =   __goal__
17. lane   - /ā/ + /ō/ =   __loan or lone__

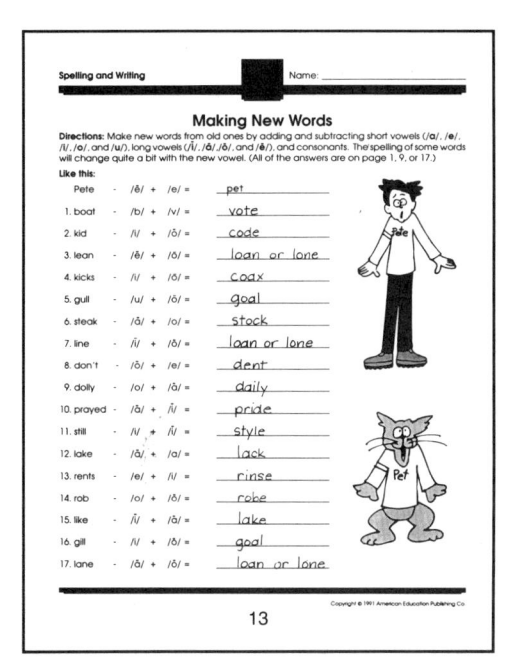

13

Finishing A Crossword Puzzle

Directions: Write the word to match each definition in the spaces that start with the same number. (If you are having trouble spelling the words, they are in the word box on page 17.)

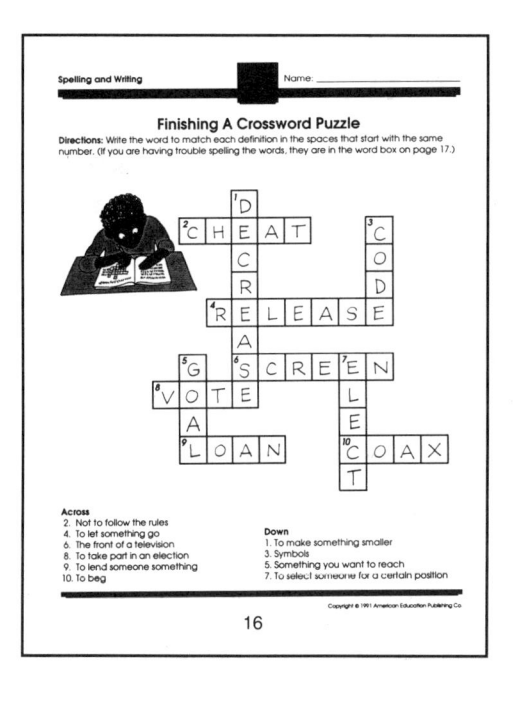

Crossword answers:
- 2 Across: CHEAT
- 4 Across: RELEASE
- 6 Across: SCREEN
- 8 Across: VOTE
- 9 Across: LOAN
- 10 Across: COAX
- 1 Down: DECREASE
- 3 Down: CODE
- 5 Down: GOAL
- 7 Down: ELECT

Across
2. Not to follow the rules
4. To let something go
6. The front of a television
8. To take part in an election
9. To lend someone something
10. To beg

Down
1. To make something smaller
3. Symbols
5. Something you want to reach
7. To select someone for a certain position

16

Review

Directions: Pretend your school is going to vote on new school colors. The grade four class wants one set of colors, maybe blue and gold, but your class wants different colors. Follow these steps to write a story about this election.

Step One: On another sheet of paper, write your ideas about what might happen. How could your class convince other classes to vote for the colors you want? What might the grade four class do to get students to vote for their colors?

Step Two: Look over your ideas and pick those you want to use in your story. Put them in order so your story has a beginning (explaining the situation), a middle (telling what everyone did), and an end (showing how the election turned out and how everyone felt about it).

Step Three: Write your story in sentences.
A. Include at least six of these words: release, elect, loan, coax, cheat, screen, vote, decrease, code, goal.
B. Use adjectives and adverbs to help explain what happens.
C. Use specific words instead of general ones.
D. Use both "plain" verbs and the -ing forms (with is, are, was, or were).

Step Four: Read your story out loud to a partner and listen while your partner reads his or hers. Are both stories clear? Did either of you leave anything out? Did you use specific words?

Step Five: Make any needed changes and rewrite your story below. Give it a title. Use more paper if you need it. Maybe your teacher will post the stories on the wall or bulletin board so you can read each others' and find out what happened in all the elections.

stories will vary

Cracking The Code

Directions: Each symbol below stands for a consonant letter. Write the letters on the lines under each symbol. Then add vowels to spell words from the word box.

| challenge | shock | thaw | chart | threaten | perish | chill | shiver | thrive | shield |

| ☆ | + | ○ | × | ∑ | □ | ● | π | § | ★ | = |
| c | d | g | h | k | l | n | p | r | s | t | ø | v | w |

Like this:
☆ × ☆ =
s h c k → shock

1. ø × = → thaw
2. ☆ × ● ● → chill
3. ☆ × ● × → shiver
4. □ × ☆ × → perish
5. ☆ × ● + → shield
6. ☆ × ● + → chart
7. = × ● × → thrive
8. ø × § × = × → threaten
9. ☆ × ● ● ○ → challenge

Spelling Words With Digraphs

A digraph is two consonant letters pronounced as one consonant sound. Here are three digraphs: /sh/ as in **sh**ell, /ch/ as in **ch**ew, and /th/ as in **th**in.

Directions: Write in **sh**, **ch**, or **th** to complete each word below.

1. **th** reaten
2. **ch** ill
3. **sh** ock
4. **sh** iver
5. **th** aw
6. **ch** allenge
7. peri **sh**
8. **sh** ield
9. **ch** art
10. **th** rive

Directions: Finish these sentences with a word that contains the digraph given.

1. A trip to the South Pole would really be a /ch/ **challenge**.
2. The ice there never /th/ **thaws** because the temperature averages -50 C.
3. How can any living thing /th/ **thrive** or even live when it's so cold?
4. With six months of total darkness and those icy temperatures, any plants would soon /sh/ **perish**.
5. Even the thought of that numbing cold makes me /sh/ **shiver**.
6. The cold and darkness /th/ **threaten** the lives of explorers.
7. The explorers take along maps and /ch/ **charts** to help them find their way.
8. Special clothing helps protect and /sh/ **shield** them from the cold.
9. Still, the weather must be a /sh/ **shock** at first.
10. Did someone leave a door open? Suddenly I feel a /ch/ **chill**.

Combining Ideas

When two sentences repeat some of the same information, we often can combine them into one sentence with fewer words.

Directions: Combine each set of sentences into one sentence. Some will have two subjects, some will have two verbs, and some will be joined with words such as **when**, **before**, **but**, or **because**.

Like this: The sun came out. The river started to thaw. The pond also thawed.
When the sun came out, the river and pond started to thaw.

1. The rain continued for days. The river flooded. The river threatened to cover the roads.
When the rain continued for days, the river flooded and threatened to cover the roads.

2. The catcher shivered in the cold morning air. The batter shivered, too. They had forgotten their jackets.
The catcher and batter shivered in the cold morning air because they had forgotten their jackets.

3. I talked to my plants. I watered them every day. They still died.
I talked to my plants and watered them every day, but they still died.

4. Germs thrive on dirty hands. Bacteria thrive, too. They both multiply there.
Germs and bacteria thrive and multiply on dirty hands.

Directions: Write your own sentences, following the instructions. _sentences will vary_
1. Write a sentence with two subjects:
2. Write a sentence with two verbs:
3. Write a sentence with two subjects and two verbs:

Choosing "Joining Words"

Too many short sentences make writing seem choppy, but we can combine some of these sentences with "joining words."

Directions: Use one of the "joining words" given to combine each pair of sentences.

Like this:
or / but / before — I was wearing my winter coat. I started to shiver.
I was wearing my winter coat, but I started to shiver.

when / but / and — Animals all need water. They may perish without it.
Animals all need water, and they may perish without it.

after / or / but — 2. The sun came out. The ice began to thaw.
After the sun came out, the ice began to thaw.

and / but / because — 3. The sun came out. The day was still chilly.
The sun came out, but the day was still chilly.

but / when / or — 4. Will the flowers perish? Will they thrive?
Will the flowers perish or will they thrive?

or / when / but — 5. The bear came closer. We began to feel threatened.
When the bear came closer, we began to feel threatened.

but / because / before — 6. Winning was a challenge. Our team didn't have much experience.
Winning was a challenge because our team didn't have much experience.

but / because / before — 7. Winning was a challenge. Our team was up to it.
Winning was a challenge, but our team was up to it.

Directions: Write three sentences of your own. Use one of these joining words in each sentence: and, but, or, when, after, because, so, before.
sentences will vary.

Searching For Synonyms

Directions: Circle a word or a phrase in each sentence that is a synonym for a word in the word box. Write the synonym from the word box on the line.

| challenge | shock | thaw | chart | frighten | perish | chill | shiver | thrive | shield |

Like this: The writing was in an (old) code. _ancient_

1. A fish out of water will quickly (die). _perish_
2. The ice carving is beginning to (melt). _thaw_
3. I was (amazed) when I saw how he looked. _shocked_
4. The puppy was (trembling) with excitement. _shivering_
5. Ferns need moisture to (grow well). _thrive_
6. Are you trying to (scare) me? _frighten_
7. Let the salad (get cold) in the refrigerator. _chill_
8. She tried to (protect) him from the truth. _shield_
9. He made a (list) of different kinds of birds. _chart_
10. They (dared) us to enter the contest. _challenged_

Directions: Write your own sentences for five words from the word box to prove you know what they mean. (If you're not sure of a word's meaning, look it up or ask someone else. Do you think that person understands the words he or she used in sentences?)

sentences will vary

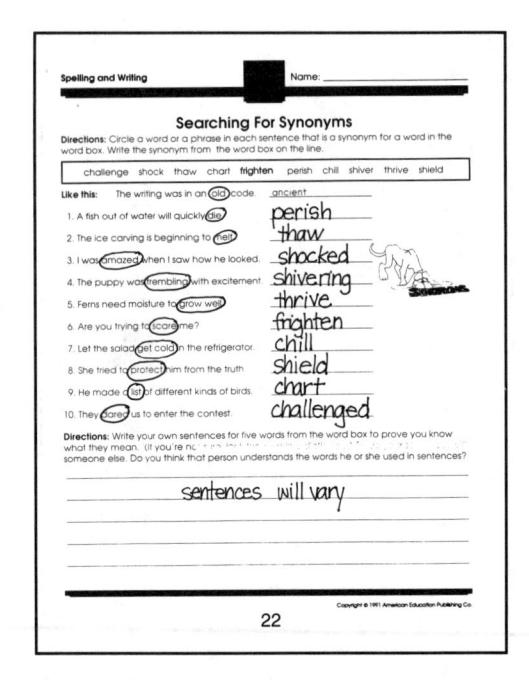

Knowing When To Stop

Although we can combine some of our short sentences, we also need to know when to end a sentence and start a new one.

Directions: Use periods, question marks, and exclamation marks to show where sentences should end in these paragraphs. Circle the first letter in the first word of each new sentence to show if it should be a capital letter.

(T)he farmers were worried about their orange crop. (T)emperatures that night were supposed to reach a record low. (T)he chill might stop the buds on the trees from developing into oranges(.) (T)he drop in temperature threatened to ruin the entire year's crop.

(O)n our last camping trip I was really glad to have my new sleeping bag(.) (T)he other campers were shivering in their sleeping bags, but mine had a special lining that shielded me from the cold(.) (T)he next morning I noticed ice on a puddle starting to thaw(.) (I) was shocked(.) (I) really had been cold that night(.) (T)hank goodness for my new sleeping bag!

Directions: Some of the periods in the paragraphs below are in the wrong place. Rewrite each paragraph, putting periods where they belong and combining some of the shorter sentences.

The Antarctic Circle. Is the area around the South Pole. Days there are six months long. Nights are also six months long. When it is day at the South Pole. It is night at the North Pole.

The Antarctic Circle is the area around the South Pole. Days and nights are six months long. When it is day at the South Pole, it is night at the North Pole.

Some people think tourists should not go into the Antarctic Circle. Because they disturb the animals that live there. Tours tend to take place. At the same time the penguins begin their breeding season. The seals also breed then. Sometimes the animals leave the breeding areas. When they feel threatened by tourists. They also are scared of the tourists' helicopters.

Some people think tourists should not go into the Antarctic Circle because they disturb the animals that live there. Tours tend to take place at the same time the penguins and seals begin their breeding season. Sometimes the animals leave the breeding areas when they feel threatened by tourists and their helicopters.

23

Practicing Proofreading

Directions: Circle the six spelling and pronoun mistakes in each paragraph. Write the words correctly on the lines below. (Some words are from earlier lessons. If you have trouble spelling them, look on page 1, 9, 17, or 25.)

Julie always (bragd) about being ready to (meat) any (chalenge) or reach any (gole). When it was time for our class to (elekt) (it) new officers, Julie said we should (vot) for her to be president.

| bragged | challenge | goal |
| elect | its | vote |

Gary wanted to be (our) president, too. He tried to (coaks) everyone to vote for (his). He even (lowned) kids money to get their votes! Well, Julie may have too much (pryde) in herself, but I like her in (spit) of that. At least she didn't try to buy our votes!

| our | coax | him |
| loaned | pride | spite |

(It's) true that Julie tried other ways to get us to vote for (hers). She (scrubed) the chalkboards even though it was my (dayly) job for that week. One day I saw her (rinseing) out the paint brushes when it was Peter's turn to do it. Then she made sure we knew about her good deeds so we would (praze) her.

| It's | her | scrubbed |
| daily | rinsing | praise |

We had the election, but I was (shakked) when the teacher (releeseed) the results. Gary won! I wondered if he (cheeted) somehow. I feel like our class was (robed)! Now Gary is the one who (braging) about how great he is. I wish he knew the (titel) of president doesn't mean anything if no one wants to be around you!

| shocked | released | cheated |
| robbed | bragging | title |

24

Review

The temperature at the North Pole averages -20 to -30 degrees F in the winter and approaches the melting point only during June, July, and August. Snow and ice cover the land the rest of the year, and the seas are choked with ice. The first people to reach the North Pole, U.S. explorers Robert E. Peary and Matthew Henson, traveled there by dog sled in 1909. Many other explorers died trying to reach this spot.

Directions: Write a story about something that might have happened as Peary and Henson struggled to the North Pole so long ago. Were they threatened by any dangerous animals? (Polar bears live and hunt at the North Pole.) Did they have any trouble with their dogs or their food supply or the weather? Use your own paper if necessary.

Follow these steps:
Step One: Write all your ideas for a story on another sheet of paper. Then pick the ones you want to use and put them in order.
Step Two: Write your story in sentences on another sheet of paper.
A. Include at least six of these words: challenge, shock, thaw, chart, threaten, perish, chill, shiver, thrive, shield.
B. Combine some of your short sentences using joining words.
C. Use periods, questions marks, exclamation marks, and capital letters in your sentences.
Step Three: Read your story out loud to a partner. Help each other by suggesting changes that will make your stories easier to understand. Is it clear what happened in your stories?
Step Four: Rewrite your story in the space below. Use more paper if you need it. If you want, draw a picture to go with it. Perhaps your teacher will have a few students read their stories every day so you can all enjoy the imaginary adventures of Peary and Henson.

Stories will vary

25

Writing Support Sentences For A Topic

A paragraph is a group of sentences that tell about one topic. The topic sentence in a paragraph usually is first and tells the main idea of the paragraph. Support sentences follow and provide details about the same topic.

Directions: Write at least three support sentences for each topic sentence below. Use your imagination, but make sure each of your sentences is on the same topic. (Some sentences offer a choice of topics. Underline the one you like best and write about it.)

Like this:
Carly had an accident on her bike. She was on her way to the store to buy some bread. A car came weaving down the road and scared her. She rode her bike off the road so the car wouldn't hit her. Now her knee is scraped, but she's all right.

I've been thinking of ways I could make some money after school.

support sentences will vary

_____
_____
_____

In my opinion, cats (or dogs or fish) make the best pets.
_____
_____
_____

My life would be better if I had (a younger sister, a younger brother, an older sister, or an older brother).
_____
_____
_____

I'd like to live next door to a (swimming pool or video store or movie theater).
_____
_____
_____

26

Sounding Out Syllables

A syllable is a word or part of a word with only one vowel. For example, **boat** has one syllable, **ta-ble** has two syllables, **re-mem-ber** has three syllables, and **ex-pe-ri-ence** has four syllables.

Directions: Use words from the word box in these exercises.

| decision | division | pressure | addition | ancient |
| subtraction | confusion | multiplication | social | correction |

1. Write each word from the word box in the row that tells how many syllables it has.

Two: pressure   social   ancient   _____
Three: decision   division   addition   subtraction
       confusion   correction
Five: multiplication

2. Write in the missing syllables for each word.

so cial   sub t r a c tion   mul t i p l i c a tion   pre ss u re
di v i sion   an c i ent   deci s i on   ad d i tion
c o n fusion   cor r e c tion

3. Beside each word below, write a word from the word box with the same number of syllables as it. Use each word from the word box only once.

daily	any 2-syllable word	challenging	any 3-syllable word
syllable	any 3-syllable word	election	any 3-syllable word
decreasing	any 3-syllable word	threaten	any 2-syllable word
advantage	any 3-syllable word	shivering	any 3-syllable word
title	any 2-syllable word	experimenting	multiplication

27

Putting Ideas In Order

Directions: Read each topic sentence and the ideas below it. Then put the ideas in order and write a paragraph for each topic. At least one idea doesn't belong with the rest in the same paragraph. Cross it out and don't include it in your paragraph. You can add other words or sentences to the paragraph, as long as you stay on the same topic. Begin sentences with capital letters and end them with periods, question marks, or exclamation marks. (Don't keep repeating "they" in your second paragraph. Think of other words to use.)

Like this: Topic sentence: Whales are more like people than fish.
Ideas: breathe through lungs
have skin, not scales
can drown
air goes out through blowhole
used to be hunted and killed

Whales are more like people than fish. They have skin like people instead of scales like fish. They also breathe through lungs and can drown if they stay under water too long. They breathe through a blowhole in the top of their heads.

Topic sentence: Addition is not difficult to do.
Ideas: write the answer under the line
add the third number to that
here is how to add three numbers
my math teacher is Mr. Herman
first, write the numbers in a column and put a line under the last one
then start at the top and add the first two numbers

Addition is not difficult to do. Here is how to add three numbers. First, write the numbers in a column and put a line under the last one. Then start at the top and add the first two numbers. Add the third number to that. Write the answer under the line.

Omit: my math teacher is Mr. Herman.

28

Meeting Word Families

Spelling and Writing — Name: _____

A word family is a group of words based on the same word. For example, **playful**, **playground**, and **playing** are all based on the word **play**.

Directions: Use words from the word box in these exercises.

decision	division	pressure	addition	ancient
subtraction	confusion	multiplication	social	correction

1. Write the word from the word box that belongs to the same word family as each one below.

correctly	_correction_	confused	_confusion_
divide	_division_	subtracting	_subtraction_
pressing	_pressure_	society	_social_
multiply	_multiplication_	decide	_decision_
added	_addition_	ancestor	_ancient_

2. Complete each sentence by writing the correct form of the word given. Remember to drop the final **e** on verbs before adding **-ing** or **-ed**.

Like this:
Have you (decide) _decided_ what to do? Did you make a (decide) _decision_ yet?

I am (add) _adding_ the numbers right now. Would you check my (add) _addition_ ?

This problem has me (confuse) _confused_. Can you clear up my (confuse) _confusion_ ?

This is a (press) _pressing_ problem. We feel (press) _pressure_ to solve it right away.

Is he (divide) _dividing_ by the right number? Will you help him with his (divide) _division_ ?

Try to answer (correct) _correctly_. Then you won't have to make any (correct) _corrections_ on your paper later on.

I am (multiply) _multiplying_ by 43. Maybe I should look at the (multiply) _multiplication_ tables.

I already (subtract) _subtracted_ six from ten. Are there any more (subtract) _subtraction_ problems to do?

29

Using Plurals In Math

Spelling and Writing — Name: _____

To make most nouns plural, we just add **s**. Except: When a noun ends with **s, ss, sh, ch,** or **x**, we add **es**: bus, buses; cross, crosses; brush, brushes; church, churches; box, boxes. When a noun ends with a consonant and **y**, we change the **y** to **i** and add **es**: berry, berries. The spelling of some plural words changes without adding **s**: man, men; mouse, mice.

Directions: Write in the correct plural or singular form of the words in these math problems. Write whether the problem requires addition, subtraction, multiplication, or division. Solve the problem!

Like this:
3 (mouse) _mice_ + 1 (mouse) _mouse_ = Type of problem: _addition_

1. 3 (box) _boxes_ – 2 (box) _boxes_ = Type of problem: _subtraction_
2. 2 (supply) _supplies_ + 5 (supply) _supplies_ = Type of problem: _addition_
3. 4 (copy) _copies_ x 2 _copies_ = Type of problem: _multiplication_
4. 6 (class) _classes_ ÷ 2 _classes_ = Type of problem: _division_
5. 5 (factory) _factories_ – 3 (factory) _factories_ = Type of problem: _subtraction_
6. 3 (daisy) _daisies_ x 3 _daisies_ = Type of problem: _multiplication_
7. 8 (sandwich) _sandwiches_ + 4 (sandwich) _sandwiches_ = Type of problem: _addition_
8. 2 (child) _children_ – 1 (child) _child_ = Type of problem: _subtraction_
9. 10 (brush) _brushes_ ÷ 5 _brushes_ = Type of problem: _division_
10. 4 (goose) _geese_ + 1 (goose) _goose_ = Type of problem: _addition_

31

Building Paragraphs

Spelling and Writing — Name: _____

Directions: Read each group of questions and the topic sentence. On another sheet of paper, write support sentences that answer each question. Use your imagination! Put the support sentences in order and copy them on this page after the topic sentence. Trade your paragraphs with someone else. How are your paragraphs the same? How are they different?

Questions: What was her decision? Why did she decide that? Why was the decision hard to make?

On her way home from school, Mariko made a difficult decision.
paragraphs will vary
_____
_____
_____

Questions: What was the confusion about? How was Charlie involved in it? What did he do to clear it up?

Suddenly, Charlie thought of a way to clear up all the confusion.
_____
_____
_____

Questions: Why did Beth feel awkward before? How does she feel now? What happened to change the way she feels?

Beth used to feel awkward at the school social activities.
_____
_____
_____

30

Review

Spelling and Writing — Name: _____

Directions: Think about the ways you use — or will use — addition, subtraction, multiplication, and division in your daily life. Decide which of the four you think is — or will be — the most valuable for you. Which do you think will be the least valuable? Now write two paragraphs below. In the first one, explain why you think one of the ways to work with numbers, addition for example, is or will be important in your life. In the second paragraph, tell why you think you won't need one of the ways, maybe division, very often. To write your paragraphs, follow these steps:

Step One: On another sheet of paper write down all your reasons why one form of arithmetic is useful to you. On a second sheet, write why another form may not be so useful. Read over your ideas, select the ones you want to use for each paragraph, and put them in order.

Step Two: Write both paragraphs in sentences on still another sheet of paper.
A. Begin each paragraph with a topic sentence and add details in support sentences.
B. Include at least six of these words in your paragraphs: decision, division, pressure, addition, ancient, subtraction, confusion, multiplication, social, correction.
C. Use at least six plural nouns, spelled correctly.

Step Three: Read your paragraphs to a partner. Do all the sentences belong where you put them? Would a different order make the sentences easier to understand?

Step Four: Rewrite both paragraphs in the space below. Use more paper if you need it. Or write them on a separate sheet of paper so your teacher can post everyone's opinions on a bulletin board and you can read each others'.

paragraphs will vary
_____
_____
_____
_____
_____
_____

32

Spelling and Writing

Name: _____

Review

Directions: Pretend your school is going to vote on new school colors. The grade four class wants one set of colors, maybe blue and gold, but your class wants different colors. Follow these steps to write a story about this election:

Step One: On another sheet of paper write your ideas about what might happen. How could your class convince other classes to vote for the colors you want? What might the grade four class do to get students to vote for their colors?

Step Two: Look over your ideas, and pick those you want to use in your story. Put them in order so your story has a beginning (explaining the situation), a middle (telling what everyone did), and an end (showing how the election turned out and how everyone felt about it).

Step Three: Write your story in sentences.
A. Include at least six of these words: release, elect, loan, coax, cheat, screen, vote, decrease, code, goal.
B. Use adjectives and adverbs to help explain what happens.
C. Use specific words instead of general ones.
D. Use both "plain" verbs and the **-ing** forms (with **is, are, was,** or **were**).

Step Four: Read your story out loud to a partner and listen while your partner reads his or hers. Are both stories clear? Did either of you leave anything out? Did you use specific words?

Step Five: Make any needed changes and rewrite your story below. Give it a title. Use more paper if you need it. Maybe your teacher will post the stories on the wall or bulletin board so you can read each others' and find out what happened in all the elections.

_____

_____

_____

_____

_____

_____

_____

_____

17

Copyright © 1994 American Education Publishing Co.

Spelling and Writing

Name: _____

Spelling Words With Digraphs

A digraph is two consonant letters pronounced as one sound. Here are three digraphs: /**sh**/ as in **shell**, /**ch**/ as in **chew**, and /**th**/ as in **thin**.

Directions: Write in **sh**, **ch**, or **th** to complete each word below.

1. __ __ reaten
2. __ __ ill
3. __ __ ock
4. __ __ iver
5. __ __ aw

6. __ __ allenge
7. peri __ __
8. __ __ ield
9. __ __ art
10. __ __ rive

Directions: Finish these sentences with a word that contains the digraph given.

1. A trip to the South Pole would really be a /ch/ _____ .

2. The ice there never /th/ _____ because the temperature averages -50 C.

3. How can any living thing /th/ _____ or even live when it's so cold?

4. With six months of total darkness and those icy temperatures, any plants would soon /sh/ _____ .

5. Even the thought of that numbing cold makes me /sh/ _____ .

6. The cold and darkness /th/ _____ the lives of explorers.

7. The explorers take along maps and /ch/ _____ to help them find their way.

8. Special clothing helps protect and /sh/ _____ them from the cold.

9. Still, the weather must be a /sh/ _____ at first.

10. Did someone leave a door open? Suddenly I feel a /ch/ _____ .

Spelling and Writing

Name: _____

Choosing "Joining Words"

Too many short sentences make writing seem choppy, but we can combine some of these sentences with "joining words."

Directions: Use one of the "joining words" given to combine each pair of sentences.

Like this:

or
but
before

I was wearing my winter coat. I started to shiver.

I was wearing my winter coat, but I started to shiver.

when
but
and

1. Animals all need water. They may perish without it.

_____

after
or
but

2. The sun came out. The ice began to thaw.

_____

and
but
because

3. The sun came out. The day was still chilly.

_____

but
when
or

4. Will the flowers perish? Will they thrive?

_____

or
when
but

5. The bear came closer. We began to feel threatened.

_____

but
because
before

6. Winning was a challenge. Our team didn't have much experience.

_____

but
because
before

7. Winning was a challenge. Our team was up to it.

_____

Directions: Write three sentences of your own. Use one of these joining words in each sentence: **and, but, or, when, after, because, so, before.**

_____

_____

_____

Copyright © 1994 American Education Publishing Co.

Spelling and Writing

Cracking The Code

Directions: Each symbol below stands for a consonant letter. Write the letters on the lines under each symbol. Then add vowels to spell words from the word box.

| challenge | shock | thaw | chart | threaten | perish | chill | shiver | thrive | shield |

☆	+	○	X	Σ	□	◊	△	§	#	Ø	π	=
c	d	g	h	k	l	n	p	r	s	t	v	w

Like this:

#	X	☆	Σ
s	h	c	k

1. Ø X =
2. ☆ X □ □
3. # X π §
4. △ § # X
5. # X □ +
6. ☆ X § Ø
7. Ø X § π
8. Ø X § Ø ◊
9. ☆ X □ □ ◊ ○

shock
_____
_____
_____
_____
_____
_____
_____
_____
_____

Spelling and Writing

Name: _____

Combining Ideas

When two sentences repeat some of the same information, we often can combine them into one sentence with fewer words.

Directions: Combine each set of sentences into one sentence. Some will have two subjects, some will have two verbs, and some will be joined with words such as **when, before, but**, or **because**.

Like this: The sun came out. The river started to thaw. The pond also thawed.

When the sun came out, the river and pond started to thaw.

1. The rain continued for days. The river flooded. The river threatened to cover the roads.
_____
_____

2. The catcher shivered in the cold morning air. The batter shivered, too. They had forgotten their jackets.
_____
_____

3. I talked to my plants. I watered them every day. They still died.
_____
_____

4. Germs thrive on dirty hands. Bacteria thrive, too. They both multiply there.
_____
_____

Directions: Write your own sentences, following the instructions.

1. Write a sentence with two subjects:
_____

2. Write a sentence with two verbs:
_____

3. Write a sentence with two subjects and two verbs:
_____

21

Copyright © 1994 American Education Publishing Co.

Spelling and Writing

Name: _____

Searching For Synonyms

Directions: Circle a word or a phrase in each sentence that is a synonym for a word in the word box. Write the synonym from the word box on the line.

| challenge | shock | thaw | chart | frighten | perish | chill | shiver | thrive | shield |

Like this: The writing was in an (old) code.   ancient

1. A fish out of water will quickly die. _____

2. The ice carving is beginning to melt. _____

3. I was amazed when I saw how he looked. _____

4. The puppy was trembling with excitement. _____

5. Ferns need moisture to grow well. _____

6. Are you trying to scare me? _____

7. Let the salad get cold in the refrigerator. _____

8. She tried to protect him from the truth. _____

9. He made a list of different kinds of birds. _____

10. They dared us to enter the contest. _____

Directions: Write your own sentences for five words from the word box to prove you know what they mean. (If you're not sure, look them up in a dictionary.) Trade your sentences with someone else. Do you think that person understands the words he or she used in sentences?

_____
_____
_____
_____
_____

Copyright © 1994 American Education Publishing Co.

Knowing When To Stop

Although we can combine some of our short sentences, we also need to know when to end a sentence and start a new one.

Directions: Use periods, question marks, and exclamation marks to show where sentences should end in these paragraphs. Circle the first letter in the first word of each new sentence to show it should be a capital letter.

(T)he farmers were worried about their orange crop. temperatures that night were supposed to reach a record low the chill might stop the buds on the trees from developing into oranges the drop in temperature threatened to ruin the entire year's crop

on our last camping trip I was really glad to have my new sleeping bag the other campers were shivering in their sleeping bags, but mine had a special lining that shielded me from the cold the next morning I noticed ice on a puddle starting to thaw I was shocked it really had been cold that night thank goodness for my new sleeping bag

Directions: Some of the periods in the paragraphs below are in the wrong place. Rewrite each paragraph, putting periods where they belong and combining some of the shorter sentences.

The Antarctic Circle. Is the area around the South Pole. Days there are six months long. Nights are also six months long. When it is day at the South Pole. It is night at the North Pole.

_____

_____

Some people think tourists should not go into the Antarctic Circle. Because they disturb the animals that live there. Tours tend to take place. At the same time the penguins begin their breeding season. The seals also breed then. Sometimes the animals leave the breeding areas. When they feel threatened by tourists. They also are scared of the tourists' helicopters.

_____

_____

_____

Spelling and Writing

Name: _____

Practicing Proofreading

Directions: Circle the six spelling and pronoun mistakes in each paragraph. Write the words correctly on the lines below. (Some words are from earlier lessons. If you have trouble spelling them, look on page 3, 11, or 18.)

    Julie always braged about being ready to meet any chalenge or reach any gole. When it was time for our class to elekt it's new officers, Julie said we should voat for her to be president.

_____ _____ _____

_____ _____ _____

    Gary wanted to be ours president, too. He tried to coaks everyone to vote for his. He even lowned kids money to get their votes! Well, Julie may have too much pryde in herself, but I like her in spit of that. At least she didn't try to buy our votes!

_____ _____ _____

_____ _____ _____

    Its true that Julie tried other ways to get us to vote for hers. She scrubed the chalkboards even though it was my dayly job for that week. One day I saw her rinseing out the paint brushes when it was Peter's turn to do it. Then she made sure we knew about her good deeds so we would praize her.

_____ _____ _____

_____ _____ _____

    We had the election, but I was shalked when the teacher releaseed the results. Gary won! I wondered if he cheeted somehow. I feel like our class was robed! Now Gary is the one who's braging about how great he is. I wish he knew the titel of president doesn't mean anything if no one wants to be around you!

_____ _____ _____

_____ _____ _____

Spelling and Writing

Name: _____

Review

The temperature at the North Pole averages -20 to -30 degrees F in the winter and approaches the melting point only during June, July, and August. Snow and ice cover the land the rest of the year, and the seas are choked with ice. The first people to reach the North Pole, U.S. explorers Robert E. Peary and Matthew Henson, traveled there by dog sled in 1909. Many other explorers died trying to reach this spot.

Directions: Write a story about something that might have happened as Peary and Henson struggled to the North Pole so long ago. Were they threatened by any dangerous animals? (Polar bears live and hunt at the North Pole.) Did they have any trouble with their dogs or their food supply or the weather? Use your own paper if necessary.

Follow these steps:
Step One: Write all your ideas for a story on another sheet of paper. Then pick the ones you want to use and put them in order.
Step Two: Write your story in sentences on another sheet of paper.
A. Include at least six of these words: challenge, shock, thaw, chart, threaten, perish, chill, shiver, thrive, shield.
B. Combine some of your short sentences using joining words.
C. Use periods, questions marks, exclamation marks, and capital letters in your sentences.
Step Three: Read your story out loud to a partner. Help each other by suggesting changes that will make your stories easier to understand. Is it clear what happened in your stories?
Step Four: Rewrite your story in the space below. Use more paper if you need it. If you want, draw a picture to go with it. Perhaps your teacher will have a few students read their stories every day so you can all enjoy the imaginary adventures of Peary and Henson.

_____

_____

_____

_____

_____

_____

Spelling and Writing

Writing Support Sentences For A Topic

A paragraph is a group of sentences that tell about one topic. The topic sentence in a paragraph usually is first and tells the main idea of the paragraph. Support sentences follow and provide details about the same topic.

Directions: Write at least three support sentences for each topic sentence below. Use your imagination, but make sure each of your sentences is on the same topic. (Some sentences offer a choice of topics. Underline the one you like best and write about it.)

Like this:

Carly had an accident on her bike. She was on her way to the store to buy some bread. A car came weaving down the road and scared her. She rode her bike off the road so the car wouldn't hit her. Now her knee is scraped, but she's all right.

I've been thinking of ways I could make some more money after school.

_____
_____
_____

In my opinion, cats (or dogs or fish) make the best pets.

_____
_____
_____

My life would be better if I had (a younger sister, a younger brother, an older sister, or an older brother).

_____
_____
_____

I'd like to live next door to a (swimming pool or video store or movie theater).

_____
_____
_____

Spelling and Writing

Name: _____

Sounding Out Syllables

A syllable is a word or part of a word with only one vowel. For example, **boat** has one syllable, **ta-ble** has **two** syllables, **re-mem-ber** has three syllables, and **ex-pe-ri-ence** has four syllables.

Directions: Use words from the word box in these exercises.

| decision | division | pressure | addition | ancient |
| subtraction | confusion | multiplication | social | correction |

1. Write each word from the word box in the row that tells how many syllables it has.

Two: _____ _____ _____ _____

Three: _____ _____ _____ _____

_____ _____ _____ _____

Five: _____ _____ _____ _____

2. Write in the missing syllables for each word.

__ __ cial   sub __ __ __ __ tion   mul __ __ pli __ __ tion   pres __ __ __ __

di __ __ sion   an __ __ __ __ __   deci __ __ __ __   ad __ __ tion

__ __ __ fusion   cor __ __ __ tion

3. Beside each word below, write a word from the word box with the same number of syllables. Use each word from the word box only once.

daily   _____   challenging   _____

syllable   _____   election   _____

decreasing   _____   threaten   _____

advantage   _____   shivering   _____

title   _____   experimenting _____

27

Spelling and Writing

Name: _____

Putting Ideas In Order

Directions: Read each topic sentence and the ideas below it. Then put the ideas in order and write a paragraph for each topic. At least one idea doesn't belong with the rest in the same paragraph. Cross it out and don't include it in your paragraph. You can add other words or sentences to the paragraph, as long as you stay on the same topic. Begin sentences with capital letters, and end them with periods, question marks, or exclamation marks. (Don't keep repeating "they" in your second paragraph. Think of other words to use.)

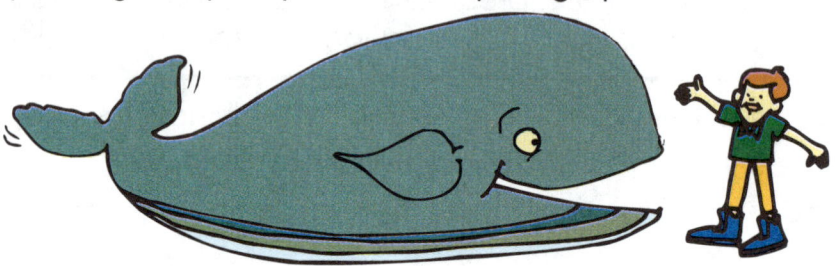

Like this:
Topic sentence: Whales are more like people than fish.
Ideas: breathe through lungs
have skin, not scales
can drown
air goes out through blowhole
used to be hunted and killed

Whales are more like people than fish. They have skin like people instead of scales like fish. They also breathe through lungs like people and can drown if they stay under water too long. They breathe through a blowhole in the top of their heads.

Topic sentence: Addition is not difficult to do.
Ideas: write the answer under the line
add the third number to that
here is how to add three numbers
my math teacher is Mr. Herman
first, write the numbers in a column and put a line under the last one
then start at the top and add the first two numbers

_____
_____
_____
_____

Spelling and Writing

Name: _____

Meeting Word Families

A word family is a group of words based on the same word. For example, **playful**, **playground**, and **playing** are all based on the word **play**.

Directions: Use words from the word box in these exercises.

decision	division	pressure	addition	ancient
subtraction	confusion	multiplication	social	correction

1. Write the word from the word box that belongs to the same word family as each one below.

correctly	_____	confused	_____
divide	_____	subtracting	_____
pressing	_____	society	_____
multiply	_____	decide	_____
added	_____	ancestor	_____

2. Complete each sentence by writing the correct form of the word given. Remember to drop the final **e** on verbs before adding **-ing** or **-ed**.

Like this:
Have you (decide) __decided__ what to do? Did you make a (decide) __decision__ yet?

I am (add) _____ the numbers right now. Would you check my (add) _____ ?

This problem has me (confuse) _____ . Can you clear up my (confuse) _____ ?

This is a (press) _____ problem. We feel (press) _____ to solve it right away.

Is he (divide) _____ by the right number? Will you help him with his (divide) _____ ?

Try to answer (correct) _____ . Then you won't have to make any (correct) _____ on your paper later on.

I am (multiply) _____ by 43. Maybe I should look at the (multiply) _____ tables.

I already (subtract) _____ six from ten. Are there any more (subtract) _____ problems to do?

Spelling and Writing

Name: _____

Building Paragraphs

Directions: Read each group of questions and the topic sentence. On another sheet of paper, write support sentences that answer each question. Use your imagination! Put the support sentences in order and copy them on this page after the topic sentence. Trade your paragraphs with someone else. How are your paragraphs the same? How are they different?

Questions: What was her decision?   Why did she decide that?
Why was the decision hard to make?

On her way home from school, Mariko made a difficult decision.

_____

_____

_____

_____

Questions: What was the confusion about?   How was Charlie involved in it?
What did he do to clear it up?

Suddenly, Charlie thought of a way to clear up all the confusion.

_____

_____

_____

Questions: Why did Beth feel awkward before?   How does she feel now?
What happened to change the way she feels?

Beth used to feel awkward at the school social activities.

_____

_____

_____

_____

Spelling and Writing

Name: _____

Using Plurals In Math

To make most nouns plural, we just add **s**, except when a noun ends with **s, ss, sh, ch**, or **x**. Add **es**: bus, bus**es**; cross, cross**es**; brush, brush**es**; church, church**es**; box, box**es**. When a noun ends with a consonant and **y**, we change the **y** to **i** and add **es**: berry, ber**ries**. The spelling of some plural words changes without adding **s**: man, men; mouse, mice.

Directions: Write in the correct plural or singular form of the words in these math problems. Write whether the problem requires addition, subtraction, multiplication, or division. Solve the problem!

Like this:

    3 (mouse) ____mice____ + 1 (mouse) ____mouse____ = Type of problem: ____addition____

1. 3 (box) _____ - 2 (box) _____ = Type of problem: _____

2. 2 (supply) _____ + 5 (supply) _____ = Type of problem: _____

3. 4 (copy) _____ × 2 (copy) _____ = Type of problem: _____

4. 6 (class) _____ ÷ 2 (class) _____ = Type of problem: _____

5. 5 (factory) _____ - 3 (factory) _____ = Type of problem: _____

6. 3 (daisy) _____ × 3 (daisy) _____ = Type of problem: _____

7. 8 (sandwich) _____ + 4 (sandwich) _____ = Type of problem: _____

8. 3 (child) _____ - 1 (child) _____ = Type of problem: _____

9. 10 (brush) _____ ÷ 5 (brush) _____ = Type of problem: _____

10. 4 (goose) _____ + 1 (goose) _____ = Type of problem: _____

Spelling and Writing

Name: _____

Review

Directions: Think about the ways you use — or will use — addition, subtraction, multiplication, and division in your daily life. Decide which of the four you think is — or will be — the most valuable for you. Which do you think will be the least valuable? Now write two paragraphs below. In the first one, explain why you think one of the ways to work with numbers, addition for example, is or will be important in your life. In the second paragraph, tell why you think you won't need one of the ways, maybe division, very often. To write your paragraphs, follow these steps:

Step One: On another sheet of paper write down all your reasons why one form of arithmetic is useful to you. On a second sheet, write why another form may not be so useful. Read over your ideas, select the ones you want to use for each paragraph, and put them in order.

Step Two: Write both paragraphs in sentences on still another sheet of paper.
A. Begin each paragraph with a topic sentence and add details in support sentences.
B. Include at least six of these words in your paragraphs: decision, division, pressure, addition, ancient, subtraction, confusion, multiplication, social, correction.
C. Use at least six plural nouns, spelled correctly.

Step Three: Read your paragraphs to a partner. Do all the sentences belong where you put them? Would a different order make the sentences easier to understand?

Step Four: Rewrite both paragraphs in the space below. Use more paper if you need it or write them on a separate sheet of paper so your teacher can post everyone's opinions on a bulletin board.

_____
_____
_____
_____
_____
_____
_____
_____

Copyright © 1994 American Education Publishing Co.